© Copyright 2015 by Charles Treft

Dedicated to my parents John and Marilyn Treft who encouraged me to "Strive for Excellence!"

It was the first day of school at the Alpaca Lane Criations Elementary School. The students were very excited to meet their new teacher, Mr. Chockablock. They had heard from other students that he had a plan for helping students get really smart.

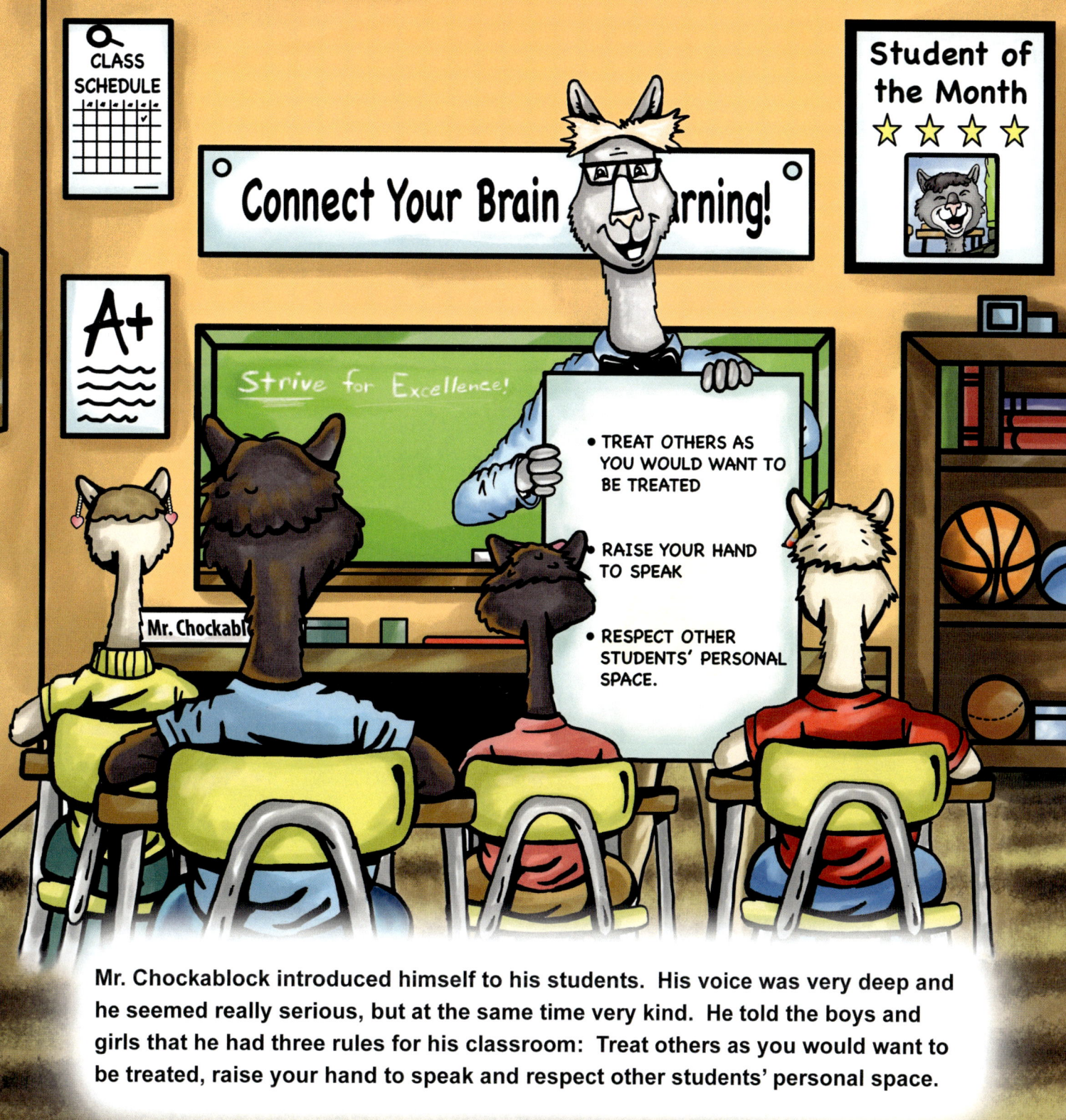

Mr. Chockablock introduced himself to his students. His voice was very deep and he seemed really serious, but at the same time very kind. He told the boys and girls that he had three rules for his classroom: Treat others as you would want to be treated, raise your hand to speak and respect other students' personal space.

Mr. Chockablock told the students he had been teaching for 15 years and that he really liked his job. He then asked the students to introduce themselves. The students introduced themselves one by one, "Hi, I am Tootsie," "Hi, I am Celeste," "Hi, I am Champ," "Hi, I am Bella."

Connect Your Brain to

Strive for Excellence!

Soon after the students introduced themselves, Mr. Chockablock asked the students who would like to get really smart this school year. Every student raised their hand. With a twinkle in his eye, Mr. Chockablock told the students he had a way for each of them to get really smart.

Tootsie, who always loved to ask questions, asked, "How can we get really smart this year?" Mr. Chockablock thanked Tootsie for being brave and asking a question. He then pointed to a piece of paper next to Tootsie's nametag.

Mr. Chockablock told the students the piece of paper was a *learning pledge*. He told the students that if they did all of the things listed on the *learning pledge*, they would get really smart this school year. Mr. Chockablock started to read the *learning pledge* to the class, "I will *Give my Best, Own my Learning…*."

Celeste asked Mr. Chockablock, "What does it mean to *Own my Learning*? Do I have to use my lunch money to buy my learning?" Mr. Chockablock chuckled, "No, no need to buy anything. Some examples of *Owning your Learning* are to be responsible by completing all of your assignments and by asking questions when you don't understand something."

Mr. Chockablock finished reading the rest of the *learning pledge* to the class. He then asked the class what they thought it meant to *Always be Ready to Learn*. Champ, who could be the class clown at times, said he thought it meant to always have his brain turned on. The class chuckled. Mr. Chockablock told the class that Champ was right, if they connected their brains to learning, they would *Always be Ready to Learn*.

Mr. Chockablock asked Champ for his help with a demonstration, so the class would understand what it meant to *Always be Ready to Learn*. Champ loved to be the center of attention, so he happily went to the front of the classroom. Mr. Chockablock handed Champ a battery. "Champ, will that battery do anything for you, if you just hold it in your hand?" asked Mr. Chockablock. "Not unless you connect it to something," said Champ. "You are right Champ!" said Mr. Chockablock.

Connect Your Brain to Learning!

Mr. Chockablock handed Champ a flashlight and told him to connect the battery. Champ connected the battery to the flashlight and then turned it on. "I think I get it Mr. Chockablock, is the battery like our brain?" asked Champ. "Yes!" said Mr. Chockablock. Champ continued, "So if our brain is *connected to learning* and turned on, it means we will *Always be Ready to Learn?*" asked Champ. "Yes, you have it Champ, students whose brains are *connected to learning* are always ready to learn and stand out in the classroom just like the light from the flashlight," said Mr. Chockablock.

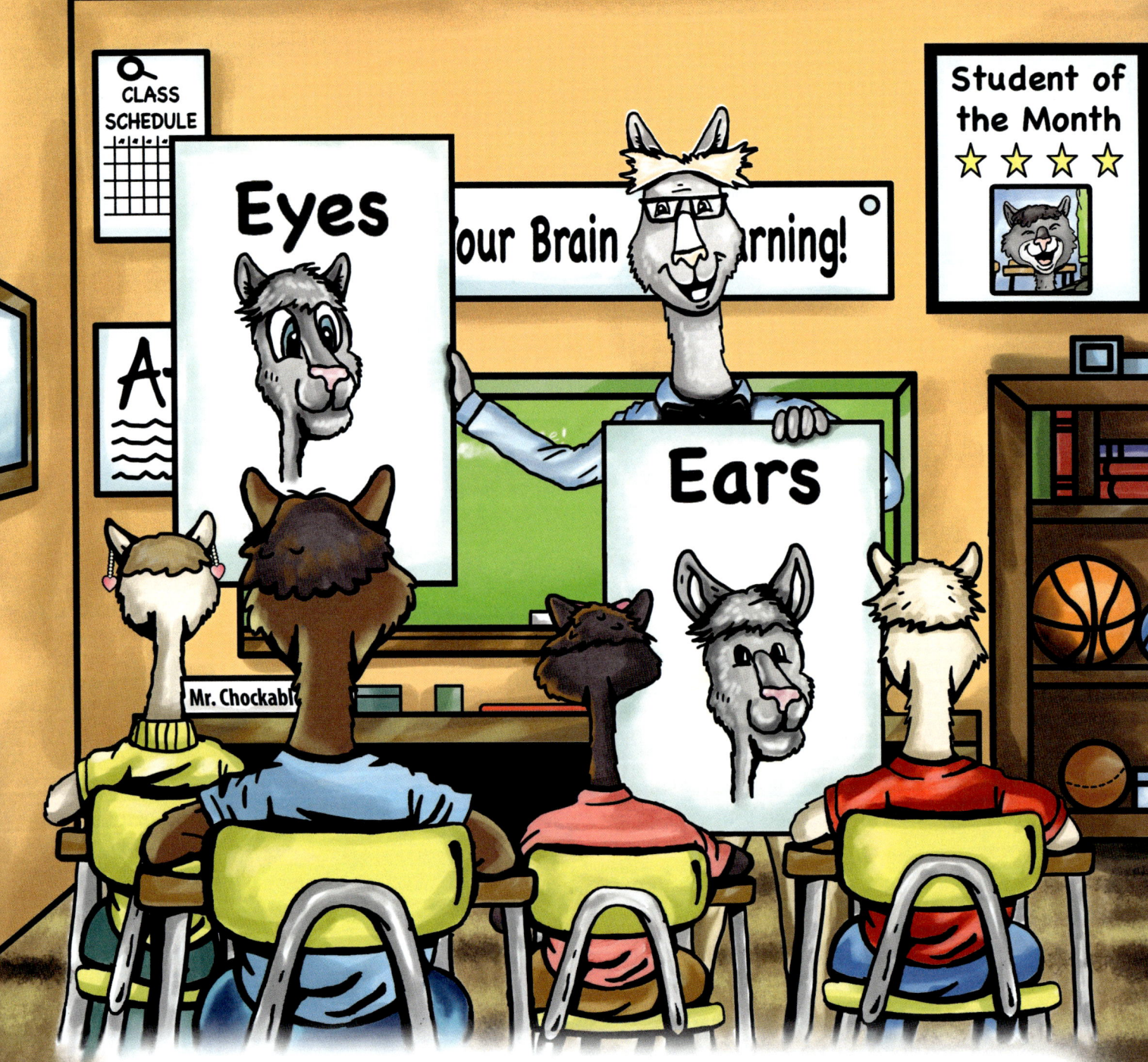

Mr. Chockablock told the class that anytime they heard him say "Ears!" or "Eyes!" it meant he had something important to tell or show them. He told the class that their "Eyes" and "Ears" would help them to *Always be Ready to Learn* and to *connect their brains to learning*.

"Boys and girls," Mr. Chockablock continued, "What does it mean to *Love to Learn*?" Champ told the class he thought that it meant to draw hearts on his paper. Tootsie said, "It means to love your teacher!" The class chuckled. Just then Mr. Chico, the principal, heard the children laughing from the hallway. He immediately walked into Mr. Chockablock's classroom to see if the students were learning. "Everything alright, Mr. Chockablock?" asked Mr. Chico. "Oh yes sir, Mr. Chico, the students are learning how to be successful in school and I am teaching them about our Learning Pledge," said Mr. Chockablock.

Mr. Chockablock asked Mr. Chico if he would tell the students what it meant to *Love to Learn*. Mr. Chico told the students that it meant they should always be looking for ways to get smarter. Champ, who couldn't resist trying to get a laugh, asked Mr. Chico if he could learn how to be the principal. Mr. Chico told Champ that if he was really serious about learning how to be a leader, he would let him be the principal for a day. Mr. Chico also told the students that *Loving to Learn* meant they could learn anywhere and not just in school. He told the students they could learn from their parents, at the supermarket, at the gas station, from television and from friends.

Mr. Chockablock asked the class who wanted to get really smart this year by *Giving their Best, Owning their Learning, Always being Ready to Learn and Loving to Learn*. Bella, Champ, Tootsie and Celeste raised their hands, Champ even raised both of his hands. Bella noticed they hadn't yet talked about *Striving for Excellence*. "Mr. Chockablock you forgot the last line of the learning pledge, we will *Strive for Excellence*," said Bella. "You are right, Bella," said Mr. Chockablock, "But, before we talk about *Striving for Excellence*, I need a volunteer to help me with one more demonstration."

Champ, of course, raised both of his hands to volunteer to help with the demonstration, but Mr. Chockablock told the class he was going to pick a student who could say the entire learning pledge. Bella, who was always listening, quickly raised her hand and recited the learning pledge for the class: *"I will….Give my Best, Own my Learning, Always be Ready to Learn, Love to Learn and Strive for Excellence."* The class gave Bella a standing ovation.

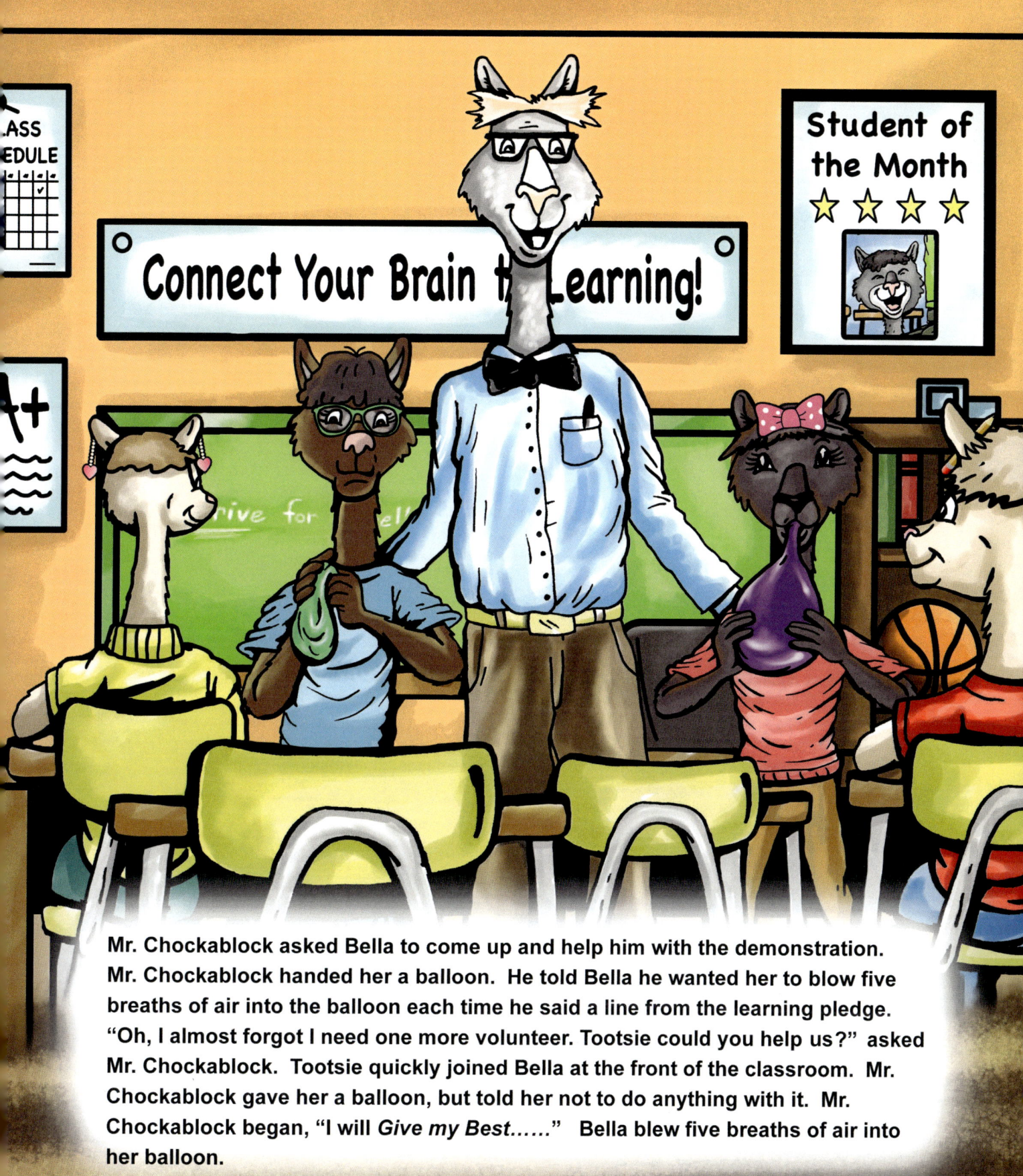

Mr. Chockablock asked Bella to come up and help him with the demonstration. Mr. Chockablock handed her a balloon. He told Bella he wanted her to blow five breaths of air into the balloon each time he said a line from the learning pledge. "Oh, I almost forgot I need one more volunteer. Tootsie could you help us?" asked Mr. Chockablock. Tootsie quickly joined Bella at the front of the classroom. Mr. Chockablock gave her a balloon, but told her not to do anything with it. Mr. Chockablock began, "I will *Give my Best......*" Bella blew five breaths of air into her balloon.

Mr. Chockablock continued, "I will *Own my Learning*, I will *Always be Ready to Learn*, I will *Love to Learn* and I will *Strive for Excellence*." Champ told the class he thought Bella's balloon was going to bust. Bella was just happy she didn't have to blow into the balloon one more time. She was out of breath.

"Class," said Mr. Chockablock, "Do you see any difference between Bella's balloon and Tootsie's balloon?" Celeste told the class that Tootsie's balloon didn't have any air in it. Mr. Chockablock told the class Celeste was right. "Students who do not *Give their Best, do not Own their Learning, are not Always Ready to Learn, do not Love to Learn and who do not Strive for Excellence* are like the balloon without any air in it. And in the end, these students don't get smart. This is very sad. But, students who *Give their Best, Own their Learning, are Always Ready to Learn, Love to Learn and Strive for Excellence* stand out and look like Bella's balloon and get really smart," said Mr. Chockablock.

Champ decided he wanted to stand out in the classroom like Bella's balloon, but he didn't really understand what it meant to *Strive for Excellence*. His soccer coach had always told him to *Give his Best*, but he had never talked to him about *Striving for Excellence*. Mr. Chockablock asked the students to look closely at the *learning pledge* to see if they could find a word they hadn't yet talked about. Almost immediately, Celeste raised her hand. "Celeste can you tell the class what word you found? asked Mr. Chockablock. "I found the word *GOALS*!" said Celeste. Mr. Chockablock asked the class if they knew what it meant to have *GOALS*. Tootsie told the class she had heard her parents talk about having *GOALS*, but she wasn't sure what the word meant. Champ told the class having *GOALS* means you want to achieve something that will help you to become successful in life.

"So, why do you think I saved *Striving for Excellence* and *GOALS* to talk about last? asked Mr. Chockablock. Bella blurted out, "I get it! Students who *Strive for Excellence* have *GOALS*!" "Yes!" said Mr. Chockablock. "If you *Give your Best*, *Own your Learning*, are *Always Ready to Learn* and *Love to Learn* you will get smart, but students who *Strive for Excellence* have a *GOAL* to become successful in life by getting really smart. Now, if you want to get really smart this school year, I want you to promise me that you will do everything on the *learning pledge* by signing your name at the bottom," said Mr. Chockablock. All of the students eagerly signed the *learning pledge*.

Mr. Chockablock posted all of the students' *learning pledges* on his bulletin board. As you probably have already guessed, Mr. Chockablock's students got really smart and were the smartest class in the entire school. Other teachers and students started asking how Mr. Chockablock's students were getting so smart. Mr. Chico asked Mr. Chockablock to go over the *learning pledge* with all of the school's students. And just as at the beginning of the school year, with a twinkle in his eye, Mr. Chockablock asked the students who wanted to get really smart and told them he had a plan. Will you get really smart this year in school?

The Learning Pledge

I will...

Give my best

Own my Learning

Always be Ready to Learn

Love to Learn

Strive for Excellence

Fun Facts About Alpacas

- Alpacas are raised for their fiber
- Alpacas will sometimes spit
- Alpacas are herd animals, so they don't like to be by themselves
- Alpacas have toes
- Alpaca babies are called crias
- Alpacas like to eat grass and grain
- Alpacas are originally from Peru, Chile and Bolivia
- Alpacas like to pronk (their form of running and jumping)
- The fiber on their head is called a topknot
- Alpacas can be 22 different colors
- Alpacas only have bottom teeth
- There are two kinds of alpacas Huacaya and Suri (have dreadlocks)
- When an alpaca lies down it is called "Cushing"
- Alpacas get shorn (fiber cut off) once a year (usually in the spring)

About the Author

Charles Treft has been an educator in public education for over eighteen years. He is currently an elementary school principal with the Calvert County Public Schools in Maryland. Charles has been a classroom teacher and vice principal at both the elementary and high school levels. Charles proudly served his country in the USMC and his community as a deputy sheriff. This is Charles's first book. The book contains messages Charles talks about each day at school with his students. Charles and his wife Susan raise alpacas, and in fact, the alpacas in the story live at their farm in Maryland. Charles wants every student to **"Strive for Excellence"** and get really smart, so they will be able to achieve their **goals** in life. Charles would love to visit your school and read his book to your students. Charles can be contacted at **CMT1962@aol.com**.

About the illustrator

Charlie J. Love

C.J. Love is a 2008 MICA (Maryland Institute College of Art) graduate and has a BFA in Graphic Design. C.J. Specializes in illustration, caricatures, mural painting, logo design, and web design. His website features his portfolio and other work. If you want to request work from him please visit **www.clove2design.com** or call him at **301-675-1643**.

Bella

Champ

Celeste

Tootsie

Mr. Chockablock

Mr. Chico

Made in the USA
Columbia, SC
02 October 2018